Starters

ANIMAL BODIES

Paws, Tails and Whiskers

by Jim Pipe

Aladdin/Watts
London • Sydney

You have a **body**.

Every animal has a **body** too.

Some animals are like you. You have two eyes and two ears. A dog does too!

4

Note to Parents and Teachers

The READING ABOUT: STARTERS series introduces key science vocabulary to young children while encouraging them to discover and understand the world around them. The series works as a set of graded readers in three levels.

in the National
one or as part of guided

rds appear in bold

hildren to use these

ll what they have read.
Below are some activities
its, carers and teachers

hildren to use specific
lp the animal to move.

compare their bodies
. raccoon, bird.

oach this by asking

flight, keeping warm,
with human skin/hair.

children to think about
animals without bones.

nagine what it's like to feel
and hedgehog (prickly).

how animals use their
ouch too.

indfold taste test!

hildren to think about
ewing or biting.

s
arly Years Teacher and
r, Westminster College,
University

Jackie Holderness – former Senior Lecturer in Primary Education, Westminster Institute, Oxford Brookes University

David Fussell – C.Chem., FRSC

CONTENTS

PAPERBACK EDITION PRINTED 2007
© Aladdin Books Ltd 2004

Designed and produced by
Aladdin Books Ltd
2/3 Fitzroy Mews
London W1T 6DF

First published in 2004
in Great Britain by
Franklin Watts
338 Euston Road
London NW1 3BH

Franklin Watts Australia
Hachette Children's Books
Level 17/207 Kent Street
Sydney NSW 2000

A catalogue record for this book is available from the British Library.
Dewey Classification: 571.1
ISBN 978 07496 7522 6

Printed in Malaysia

All rights reserved

Editor: Sally Hewitt

Design: Flick, Book Design and Graphics

Thanks to: • The pupils of Trafalgar Infants School, Twickenham • Lynne Thompson • The pupils and teachers of Trafalgar Junior School, Twickenham, and St. Nicholas C.E. Infant School, Wallingford.

Photocredits:
l-left, r-right, b-bottom, t-top, c-centre, m-middle
Front cover tl & tr, 12b, 19t, 23tr — Corel. Front cover tm & b, 3, 4, 13b, 14, 15tr, 17t, 19mr, 24 -28 all, 32tl, 32mlb — Comstock. 2tl, 6 both, 7l, 8t, 11t, 15m, 16t, 18br, 20t, 21t, 31tr, 31ml, 31mr, 32tr, 32mlt, 32mrb — Digital Stock. 2ml, 5bl, 5mr, 5br, 10t, 21ml, 22 both, 32mlc, 32mrc, 32bl, 32br — John Foxx Images. 2bl, 17br, 23b, 29 both, 30 both, 31bl — Otto Rogge Photography. 5t, 16br — Flick Smith. 7r, 12tr — Jim Pipe. 8br, 9br, 11br, 13tr, 20mr — Stockbyte. 9t, 32mrt — Dr James P. McVey/NOAA. 10br — Corbis. 18t — PBD.

Are these animals like you?
A worm has no legs.
A fish has no legs.
A bird has wings.
A snail has a shell.

Worm

Fish

Bird

Snail

• A bird flies. How do the other animals move?

You have two legs and two feet. A zebra has four legs. Its feet are **hooves**.

A tiger has four legs. Its feet are **paws**.

6

A monkey's **paws** are like hands. Its **tail** grabs like a hand too.

A monkey swings from tree to tree. Can you?

• Can your feet grab as well as your hands?

Some animals have **wings** not arms. They can fly.

A bird has two **wings**.
A dragonfly has four **wings**.

8

Sea animals have tails not legs.
Their tails push them along.

A seal steers
with its **flippers**.

A fish steers
with its **fins**.

• Which parts of your body help you swim?

Skin covers your body.
It keeps you dry.

Your **skin** feels soft. A lizard's **skin**
feels rough. It is made of **scales**.

10

Fish have smooth **scales** on their skin.
Birds have **feathers**.

Scales and **feathers**
can be bright colors.

• Why do birds have feathers?

Bones protect your insides.
They give you your shape.
Can you feel them?

Many animals have
bones too. Bird **bones**
are light for flying.

A crab has no **bones**.
A hard **shell** protects it.

A tortoise has
bones and a **shell**
on its back.

• What would you look like without bones? A jellyfish?

You have **hair** on your head.
A dog has **hairy fur** all over its body.

Fur keeps an animal warm in winter.

14

A cat has long **hairs** on its face. These are **whiskers**.

This lion has long **hairs** on his head. This is his **mane**.

• What animals would you like to stroke?

Like you, animals see with their **eyes**.
A whale's **eye** is as big as a football.

A snail has **eyes** at the end
of its **tentacles**.

16

Like you, animals hear with their **ears**.
A rabbit's long **ears** hear quiet sounds.

A grasshopper has
ears in its knees!

• Why do big ears and big eyes help night animals?

Animals smell with their **nose.**

A pig sniffs for food on the ground.

An elephant's **trunk**
is a long **nose.**
It grabs like
a hand!

Animals taste with their **tongue**. A snake smells with it too!

Animals lick food with their **tongue**. A dog has a long **tongue**.

• Shut your eyes. Can you tell food from its smell?

Sharp **teeth** are good for biting.
A shark has lots of sharp **teeth**. Crunch!

Bumpy **teeth** are good for chewing.
A cow chews grass all day. Munch!

A hippopotamus has two long **teeth**. These are its **tusks**.

Birds do not have **teeth**. They grab food with their **beak**.

• Feel your teeth. Why are some sharp and pointed?

21

Many animals have parts you don't.

Do you have **claws**?
A crab has **claws**.
Watch out, they pinch!

Do you have a **horn**? A rhino has **horns** on its head.

Watch out, it butts!

22

Do you have prickly **spines**?
A porcupine has **spines**. Watch out,
they are sharp!

A wasp has a **sting**
in its tail. Don't
make it angry!

• What other animals have parts you don't?

Now read the story of **My New Pet.** Watch for words about **animals**.

Today, we can bring
a pet to school.
I have no pet.
I want one too!

Asha has a cat called Charlie.
I'd like a cat too.
Charlie has soft **fur** and long **whiskers**.
Ouch! His **paws** have sharp **claws**.

Dave brings Goldie, his dog.
I'd like a dog too. Goldie
sniffs with his **nose**. Dave
gives him a dog biscuit.

Goldie wags his **tail**.
He sticks out his big **tongue.**
We all laugh.

Ming has a tortoise. His name is
Speedy. He moves VERY slowly.

Speedy has a tough **skin**
and a smooth **shell**.

We all look for
Speedy's **ears**.
Wow! A tortoise
does not have any!

Ben shows us his
goldfish, Moby.
I like Moby's shiny
gold **scales**.

Moby flaps his **fins**
up and down.

Moby has no **teeth**.
He just swallows his food.

Charlie's **eyes**
follow Moby.
He would like
to eat him!

Ally has a bird
called Barney.
He has white **feathers**.
"Look at his big **beak!**"
I say to Ally.

Ruth shows a picture of her pony, Rusty.
Rusty has a red **mane**.

I would like to ride Rusty.
His **hooves** go "clip-clop" on the road.

Tariq has a pet spider.
It is very **hairy**.
We count its legs.
A spider has eight legs!
It has eight **eyes** too.

I feel sad. I'd like a pet too.
My teacher says, "Come and look!"

It's a **hairy** caterpillar!
"We can watch it
grow," says my teacher.

One day, my caterpillar
will grow into a butterfly
with **wings**. Now it eats
and eats. Just like me!

Draw a picture of
your favorite animal.
Write labels to show
parts of its **body**.

Can you also draw
where it lives and
what it eats?

Tail

Ears

Paws

QUIZ

Which animal has **hooves?**

Answer on page 6

What covers a fish's **skin?**

Answer on page 11

What is a lion's **mane?**

Answer on page 15

Where are a grasshopper's **ears?**

Answer on page 17

Did you know the answers? Give yourself a

Do you remember these **animal** words?
Well done! Can you remember any more?

body
page 4

paws
page 6

wings
page 8

flippers
page 9

scales
page 10

shell
page 13

fur
page 14

trunk
page 18

beak
page 21

horn
page 22